Crafts of the World

The Art of Native American Turquoise Jewelry

Ann Stalcup

The Rosen Publishing Group's
PowerKids Press ™
New York

To my husband, Ed, who shares my love of folk art and travel

Published in 1999 by The Rosen Publishing Group, Inc.
29 East 21st Street, New York, NY 10010

First Edition

Book Design: Resa Listort

Photo Credits: pp. 4, 7, 8, 9, 11, 13, 15, 18 © Jeffrey Foxx; p. 17 © Terry Qing/FPG International; p. 19 © David McGlynn/FPG International; pp. 20-21 by Christine Innamorato.

Stalcup, Ann, 1935-
The Art of Native American Turquoise jewelry / by Ann Stalcup.
      p.   cm. — (Crafts of the world)
   Includes index.
   Summary: Discusses what turquoise is, where it's found, the types of jewelry made from it, and why the jewelry is important to Native American cultures. Includes a craft project.
   ISBN 0-8239-5332-7
   1. Indians of North America—Southwest, New—Jewelry—Juvenile literature. 2. Turquoise jewelry—Southwest, New—Juvenile literature. [1. Indians of North America—Southwest, New—Jewelry. 2. Turquoise jewelry.] I. Title. II. Series: Crafts of the world (PowerKids Press)
E78.S7S8 1998
739.27'08997079—dc21   98-5785
                                                                                              CIP
                                                                                              AC

Manufactured in the United States of America

Contents

Turquoise: A Piece of the Sky

Turquoise (TER-koyz) is a greenish-blue stone. It isn't clear like a diamond, it is **opaque** (oh-PAYK). The first turquoise was discovered in the country that we now call Iran. The turquoise found there is still the world's finest.

In the United States, turquoise is found in Arizona, Colorado, Nevada, and New Mexico. Turquoise Mountain, New Mexico, is the oldest known place to have turquoise in North America.

If copper and iron are in the ground with turquoise, they can create brownish marks in the stone. These marks are called a **matrix** (MAY-triks). The more brown there is in the turquoise, the less **valuable** (VAL-yoo-bul) it is. Many Native Americans who work with turquoise call it "a piece of the sky" because of its beautiful color.

◀ This is what turquoise looks like just after it's taken from the ground.

Native American Silversmithing

In 1850 the Navajo Indians lived in what is now New Mexico. The Navajo learned **silversmithing** (SIL-ver-SMIH-thing) from the Mexicans. Since there was a lot of turquoise in the ground where they lived, it was used to decorate silver jewelry.

In 1872 the Navajo taught silversmithing to their neighbors, the Zuni Indians. Later, the Hopi Indians also became fine silversmiths.

Today, there are many skilled jewelry makers in the southwestern United States. Silversmithing used to be done only by men. But today, some of the most famous silversmiths are women.

It takes lots of hard work and skill to make beautiful turquoise jewelry and crafts. ▶

Wearing Your Wealth

During special **ceremonies** (SEHR-eh-moh-neez), the Hopi, Navajo, and Zuni wear brightly decorated costumes. The men wear cotton pants and a cloth sash tied at the waist. The women wear long skirts. Everybody wears long-sleeved velvet shirts in rich, dark colors. Long ago, these clothes were worn every day.

For special ceremonies many Native Americans clean their turquoise jewelry, such as these rings, with suds created from a plant called the yucca.

The Native Americans of Arizona and New Mexico also "wear their wealth" during ceremonies. This means that each person wears as much turquoise and silver jewelry as he or she owns. Both men and women come to special events wearing **ornate** (or-NAYT) bracelets, rings, necklaces, and belts.

This man is showing off his beautiful silver and turquoise jewelry. ▶

Traditional Designs

Traditional (truh-DIH-shuh-nul) turquoise bracelets and belts often have designs **etched** (ECHD) into the silver. Some designs are simple shapes. Other designs show scenes from nature, such as deer, birds, and coyotes. One popular design is the squash blossom necklace. It looks like the flower from the squash plant.

The Zuni make different styles of jewelry than the Navajo. The Zuni like to use matching turquoise pieces with little or no matrix. They are very good at **inlaying** (IN-lay-ing), or setting, stones in silver.

Some silversmiths make the same designs for their bracelets, necklaces, and belts over and over again. But no two pieces are exactly the same.

These two bracelets show different patterns and designs that can be made using turquoise.

Concho Belts

   The Plains Indians used to wear silver discs called **conchos** (KON-chohz) in their hair. Concho comes from the word concha, which means shell in Spanish. The discs are called conchos because they have curved edges that look like the edges of seashells. Turquoise was often set in the conchos. The more conchos you had, the wealthier other people thought you were. Each woman wore as many as she could in her long braids.

   Today, the silver discs are often strung together and worn as belts. Many have turquoise as part of their design. The decoration and **engraving** (en-GRAY-ving) on the silver is different on each concho.

This girl is wearing turquoise in her hair, on her shirt, and on her concho belt. ▶

Fetishes

Fetishes (FEH-tih-shez) have been part of Native American life for hundreds of years. They are objects that are believed to have magical power. Turquoise is often used to make fetishes because many Native Americans believe that turquoise can get rid of evil spirits. Fetishes are usually in the shapes of animals. It is believed that an animal's spirit lives inside each fetish. That spirit offers protection to the person who carries the fetish.

People make fetishes of all different animals, but bears are the most popular fetish. ▶

14

Every animal has different powers. A hawk brings warnings, a dog stands for loyalty, and the bear stands for power and strength. Often, stone arrows called medicine bundles are tied to the back of a fetish. This makes the animal even more powerful.

Gallup Inter-Tribal Indian Ceremonial.

For four days in August, Native Americans from **reservations** (REH-zer-VAY-shunz) all over North America gather in Gallup, New Mexico. They come together for the annual ceremonial called the Gallup Inter-Tribal Indian Ceremonial. There are rodeo events, games, and traditional dances.

People also come to the ceremonial to sell their crafts. Trading posts are filled with people who want to buy or sell turquoise and silver pieces. The Native Americans look carefully at each other's work. They enjoy talking to one another about the crafts that are shown. The Indian Ceremonial is a wonderful place to see Native Americans in traditional costume wearing beautiful turquoise jewelry.

This woman is very proud of her jewelry and crafts. She hopes many people will stop to look and buy her creations. ▶

Trading Posts

Native Americans sell their turquoise jewelry, rugs, and pottery at trading posts throughout the southwestern United States. When money is needed quickly, people may **pawn** (PAWN) some of their jewelry. The trading post owner pays a fair price and puts a ticket with the owner's name on the jewelry. The owner can buy back the piece for the same price when he or she has more money. Or the owner can agree to sell it to someone else after a certain amount of time has passed.

Special pieces of turquoise jewelry, such as this necklace, can be seen at trading posts.

18

Many Native Americans store their jewelry at trading posts and pay a small amount of money to keep the jewelry safe. They pick it up whenever there is a ceremonial event. Seeing the jewelry at a trading post is like visiting a museum!

Beautiful turquoise bracelets such as ▶ these are often very expensive.

Concho Necklace or Bolo Tie:

You will need:

- a cardboard rectangle (5 inches by 4 inches)
- silver paint (spray paint works best)
- blue food coloring

- broken up eggshells from a hard-boiled egg
- a piece of heavy string or yarn (about 20 inches long)

- magic markers (any colors, but black and dark blue are best)
- scissors
- glue

1. Paint one side of the cardboard rectangle silver and let dry.

2. Paint the other side of the cardboard rectangle silver and let dry.

3. Cut out the concho shape, shown here.

4. Put eggshells in a bowl and pour a few drops of blue food coloring over them.

5. Mix the eggshells around so that they are all covered with food coloring (add food coloring a drop at a time if you need more). Let them sit in the food coloring for two to three hours, then let them dry on a paper towel.

6. Decorate the concho with markers, in any way you like.

7. Glue on the eggshells as the turquoise part of your design.

8. For concho necklace: Punch two holes in top of concho and put string through. Tie the string together at the ends.

9. For bolo tie: Punch two holes at the top of the concho and one at the bottom. Put string through the holes at the top, and then both ends of the string through the hole at the bottom.

Special Events

Fairs where turquoise jewelry is bought and sold are held throughout the year. Many of these fairs are **festivals** (FES-tih-vulz) that celebrate the importance of crops during spring and fall.

The biggest Native American fair in the Southwest is the Santa Fe Indian Market, held every August in Santa Fe, New Mexico. People show and sell their crafts at the Market. Awards are given to the best silversmiths, pottery makers, and rug makers. All the crafts at this fair are an important part of Native American **culture** (KUL-cher) and history. And they help people from all over the country learn about the beauty of the different Native American cultures.

Glossary

ceremony (SEHR-eh-moh-nee) An act or series of acts that are done on a special occasion.

concho (KON-choh) A silver disk often decorated with turquoise worn in the hair or on a belt.

culture (KUL-cher) The beliefs, customs, art, and religion of a group of people.

engraving (en-GRAY-ving) A design that is etched into metal.

etch (ECH) To carve a design into hard material such as glass or metal.

festival (FES-tih-vul) A day or special time of recognizing someone or something important.

fetish (FEH-tish) An object that is believed to have magic power.

inlay (IN-lay) To set a stone into the surface of a material such as silver.

matrix (MAY-triks) Brownish marks in turquoise that are caused by metals in the soil.

opaque (oh-PAYK) When something is so thick that light cannot pass through it.

ornate (or-NAYT) Having lots of decoration.

pawn (PAWN) To leave something in exchange for money.

reservation (REH-zer-VAY-shun) Land set aside by the government for Native Americans to live on.

silversmithing (SIL-ver-SMIH-thing) Making jewelry and crafts out of silver.

traditional (truh-DIH-shuh-nul) To do things the way a group of people has done them for a long time.

turquoise (TER-koyz) A greenish-blue stone found in Iran and the southwestern United States.

valuable (VAL-yoo-bul) Worth a lot of money.

Index